LIGHTNING
BOLT
BOOKS™

Do You Know about Mammals?

Buffy Silverman

Lerner Publications Company
Minneapolis

To Jake,
One of my
favorite mammals

Lerner Publications Company
A division of Lerner Publishing Group, Inc.
241 First Avenue North
Minneapolis, MN 55401 U.S.A.

Website address: www.lernerbooks.com

Library of Congress Cataloging-in-Publication Data

Silverman, Buffy.
    Do you know about mammals / by Buffy Silverman.
        p.   cm. — (Lightning bolt books™ – Meet the animal groups)
    Includes index.
    ISBN 978-0-8225-7539-9 (lib. bdg. : alk. paper)
    1. Mammals—Juvenile literature. I. Title.
    QL706.2.S55 2010
    599—dc22   2008008729

Manufactured in the United States of America
1 2 3 4 5 6 — BP — 15 14 13 12 11 10

Contents

Mammals Have Hair

A giraffe chews on some leaves. Her calf chews some too. A skunk sniffs beetles to eat. Her kits follow. Giraffes and skunks look different. But in some ways, they are alike. Both animals are mammals. **What are mammals?** Mammals are animals with fur or hair.

Skunks have black and white fur.

Giraffes have short fur with brown spots.

5

Squirrels are covered with fur from head to tail.

A squirrel has thick fur. It helps the squirrel stay warm in winter.

All mammals have some hair.

Elephants have hairy tails.

Mammals are endotherms. They make their own body heat. Their temperature always stays about the same. In snowy forests or sunny fields, their bodies stay warm.

A lynx sits under the hot sun. But its body temperature stays the same.

Some mammals live in frozen places. Polar bears swim in chilly waters. They run across ice. Thick fur keeps them warm.

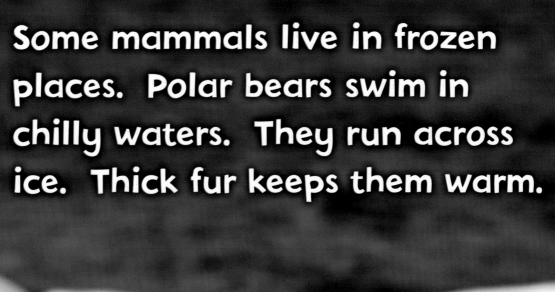

Polar bears stay warm in the coldest places.

Mountain goats climb snowy cliffs. Fur keeps their body heat inside.

Other mammals live in hot deserts. A camel's furry coat protects it from the hot sun. Desert pocket mice stay cool underground. They find food at night. It's cooler then.

Camels have fur. The fur helps them stay cool in the desert.

Baby Mammals

A mother wolf feeds her pups. This wolf pup is drinking milk. Baby mammals drink milk from their mother. Are wolves mammals? Yes! Wolves have fur, and their pups drink milk.

Wolf pups drink milk.

Most mammal babies grow inside their mothers' bodies. The babies look like their parents. Piglets look like pigs.

Piglets drink their mother's milk. Pigs are mammals.

Kangaroos give birth to babies called joeys. A joey grows in its mother's pouch. It drinks its mother's milk. Kangaroos are mammals.

A joey looks out of its mother's pouch.

15

Koalas climb into their mothers' pouches and drink milk.

At birth, koalas are the size of jelly beans. They grow bigger and look like their parents.

A few mammals lay eggs.
A platypus is a mammal that
lays eggs. After platypus eggs
hatch, the babies drink milk.
A platypus is a mammal.

Platypus babies do not have fur when they hatch. Their fur grows later.

A jackrabbit eats leaves from a tree.

What Mammals Eat

Baby mammals drink milk. They learn to eat different foods as they grow up. What do mammals eat? Beavers nibble on branches and leaves. Mammals that eat plants are called herbivores.

Beavers eat bark and leaves.

A tiger creeps close to a deer and pounces. Mammals that eat other animals are called carnivores.

This tig
caught

Opossums hunt for food at night.

Opossums feast on insects and berries. Mammals that eat both plants and animals are omnivores.

Mammals Live Everywhere

Mammals live all over the world. They live in deserts and in forests. Some mammals live in water.

Do you see hairs on this seal? Seals are sea mammals. Sea mammals have a thick layer of fat, called blubber. It keeps them warm.

Some mammals live in trees.
Spider monkeys swing from
branch to branch. They
even sleep in trees.

Spider monkeys
live in tropical
forests.

Do any mammals fly?

Bats do! Bats have fur. Their wings are made of thick skin.

Bats hunt for insects at night.

Mammals Breathe Air

Mammals live in many places.
But they all breathe air.
Dolphins breathe through a
blowhole on top of their heads.

Dolphins are mammals. They
breathe air and feed their
babies milk. Baby dolphins
have hair on their snouts.

Whales can swim underwater for more than an hour. Then they come up for air.

A whale spouts air and water from its blowhole.

All mammals have some hair or fur. Their body heat always stays about the same. Their babies drink milk.

Are you a mammal?

Find My Home

Match the mammal to its home:

beaver

camel

mountain goat

bat

whale

baby
kangaroo

human child

snow-covered mountain

kangaroo pouch

ocean

lodge in a pond

house

cave

desert

Check your answers on page 31.

Glossary

blowhole: an opening on the top of the head of a whale or dolphin for breathing

blubber: a layer of fat under the skin of whales and other sea mammals

calf: a baby giraffe

carnivore: an animal that hunts and eats other animals

endotherm: a warm-blooded animal whose body heat always stays about the same

herbivore: an animal that eats plants

joey: a baby kangaroo or koala

kit: a baby skunk

mammal: an animal that has hair, drinks its mother's milk, and whose body heat always stays about the same

omnivore: an animal that eats both plants and other animals

temperature: a measure of hotness or coldness

Further Reading

All about Mammals
http://www.kidzone.ws/animals/mammals.htm

Brownwell, M. Barbara. *Mammals.* Washington, DC: National Geographic Nature Library, 1993.

Mammals: National Geographic Kids
http://www3.nationalgeographic.com/animals/mammals.html

Small Mammals for Kids: Smithsonian National Zoological Park
http://nationalzoo.si.edu/Animals/SmallMammals/ForKids/default.cfm

Answer key for pages 28–29:
beaver – lodge in pond
camel – desert
mountain goat – snow-covered mountain
bat – cave
whale – ocean
baby kangaroo – kangaroo pouch
human child – house

Index

Photo Acknowledgments

The images in this book are used with the permission of: © Rechitan Sorin/Dreamstime.com, p. 1; © iStockphoto.com/David P. Lewis, p. 2; © Tom and Pat Leeson , p. 4; © Darrell Gulin/Stone/Getty Images, p. 5; © Photodisc/Getty Images, pp. 6, 10, 28 (goat), 29 (mountain and ocean); © Biosphoto/Crocetta Tony/Peter Arnold, Inc., p. 7; © Prisma/SuperStock, p. 8; © Daisy Gilardini/The Image Bank/Getty Images, p. 9; © iStockphoto.com/Sean Randall, pp. 11, 28 (camel), 29 (desert); © Tom Vezo/naturepl.com, p. 12; © Royalty-Free/CORBIS, pp. 13, 28 (baby); © iStockphoto.com/Nemanja Glumac, p. 14; © Theo Allofs/Visuals Unlimited, Inc., p. 15; © Daniel Cox/Oxford Scientific/Photolibrary, p. 16; © Jean-Phillipe Varin/Photo Researchers, Inc., p. 17; © John and Barbara Gerlach/Visuals Unlimited, Inc., p. 18; © Ron Spomer/Visuals Unlimited, Inc., pp. 19, 28 (beaver); © blickwinkel/Alamy, p. 20; © PhotoStockFile/Alamy, p. 21; © Pedro Diaz/Dreamstime.com, p. 22; © M. Lane/Peter Arnold, Inc., p. 23; © James Hager/Robert Harding World Imagery/Getty Images, pp. 24, 28 (bat); © Altrendo/Getty Images, p. 25; © Jeff Foott/Discovery Channel Images/Getty Images, p. 26; © Comstock Images, p. 27; © Brandon Cole/Visuals Unlimited, Inc., p. 28 (whale); © John William Banagan/Riser/Getty Images, p. 28 (kangaroo); © William Osborn/naturepl.com, p. 29 (kangaroo); © age fotostock/SuperStock, p. 29 (lodge); © Zina Seletskaya/Dreamstime.com, p. 29 (house); © Victor Zastolskiy/Dreamstime.com, p. 29 (cave); © Eriklam/Dreamstime.com, p. 30; © Devanne Philippe/Dreamstime.com, p. 31.

Front Cover: © Photodisc/Getty Images.